I0163157

My Name is William

A Collection of Stories about People who Share my Name

By Allison Dearstyne

Dedicated to every boy named William. May you grow up to be a strong protector!

The name William came from the German name Willehelm. This name comes from the roots "willeo," which means strong-willed or determined, and "helm," which means helmet or protection. So, the meaning of the name William is "determined protector."

The French variation is Guillaume, the Irish variation is Liam, and the Norman variation is William. The Norman conquest of Britain in 1066 by William the Conqueror made the name William popular in Britain. Your name has remained a favorite all over the world through the millennia!

Did you know that there are many heroes who share your name? We will look at these seven outstanding men named William who made an impact on their world:

William Kamkwamba
William Morgan
William Wilberforce
William Carney
William "Bill" Gates
William Henry Cling
William Shakespeare

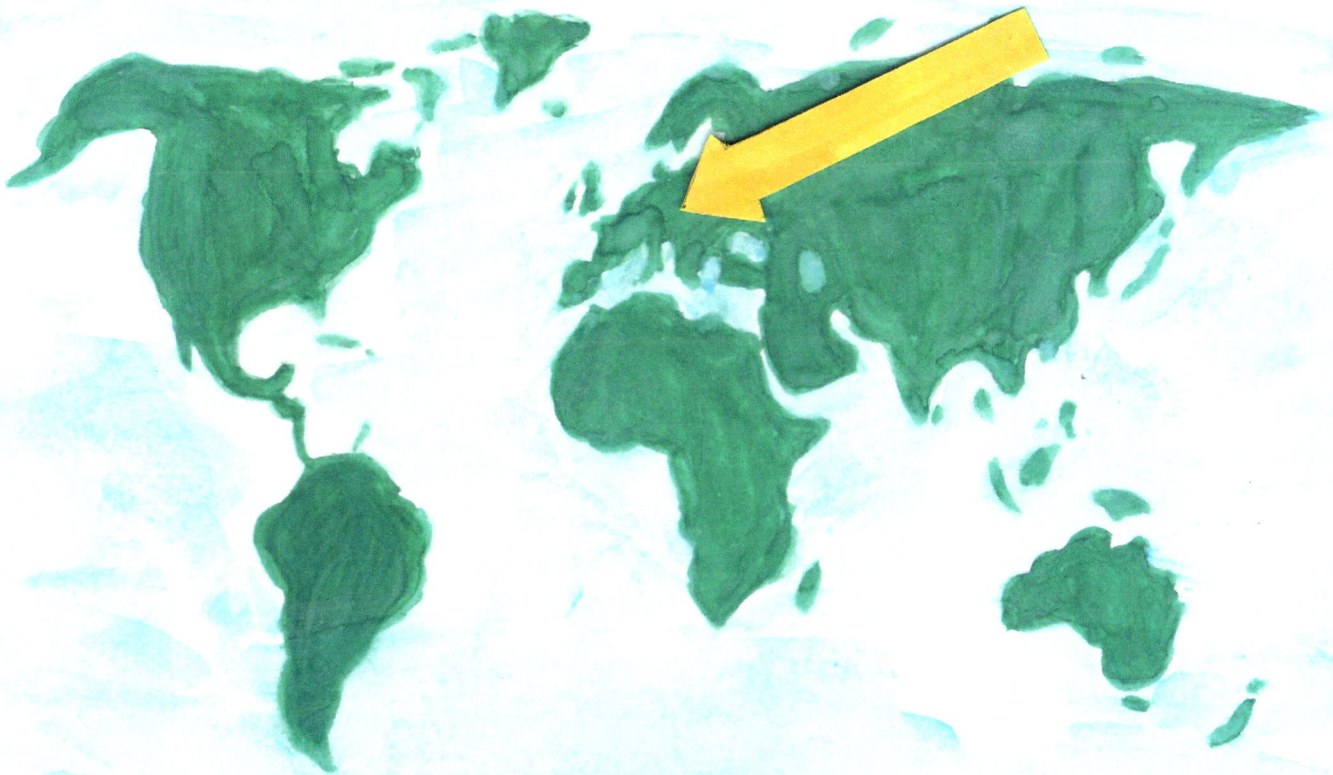

William Kamkwamba is a Malawian inventor and author. He was born in 1987 and grew up in Wimbe, a village that didn't have clean drinking water. Malnourishment and poverty were, and still are, issues that Malawi faces. William's family had to farm with tools designed hundreds of years ago to survive. As a boy, William went to school and played with recycled materials he found at a junkyard.

In 2001, Malawi experienced a terrible drought, which means that it didn't rain enough. This led to famine, which is a major food shortage. William's family lost all the season's crops, and he had to drop out of school. He desperately wanted to continue his education, so he began visiting a library. There, William discovered that he loved electronics!

One book about energy changed his life. After reading it, he decided to make a wind turbine out of whatever materials he could find. Rummaging around a local scrapyard, he collected trash that he turned into treasure. William combined bicycle parts and other metal scraps with bark from trees to create a wind turbine that powered the appliances in his house! The windmill helped his family pump the water they needed to farm.

After the famine, William wanted to return to school but his family could not afford the fee to send him. So, William snuck into school to learn in secret. Eventually he was caught, and his father begged his teachers to let him stay for a payment of his tobacco crop. His teachers agreed. Remember that your education is valuable. William knew the value of his education!

William Kamkwamba began to gain some fame in his country, and then a blog about his achievement gave him fame internationally. In 2009, he wrote an autobiography called *The Boy Who Harnessed the Wind.* It instantly became a favorite of critics. Everyone loved his story! Suddenly new opportunities arose for William. He was invited to speak at events all around Africa and he received a college scholarship. In 2014 he graduated from Dartmouth College with a degree in Environmental Studies.

All through his teenage and college years, William kept inventing. He built two more wind turbines and a solar-powered water pump! The pump provided the first clean drinking water in Wimbe and used the sun as an energy source.

William created a charity called "Moving Windmills Project." Inspired by his success story, others built low-cost, earth-friendly water wells and wind turbines throughout Malawi. They used local recycled material to make modern farm equipment to help Malawian families. A key to this wonderful organization is using African talent and training young African innovators.

TIME magazine named William one of the "30 People Under 30 Changing the World." Think about all the scraps that are thrown away in your home and think about how you might turn them into a useful invention. Then you can be like resourceful William Kamkwamba!

William Morgan was the creator of the sport volleyball. He was born in New York in 1870, and he enjoyed sports growing up. When he graduated from high school, he attended a YMCA, or Young Men's Christian Association International Training School. After graduating from college, William Morgan became the Director of Physical Education at a YMCA.

His passion was creating workout plans and teaching sports to young men. His friend James Naismith had recently invented the sport basketball, which became instantly popular among young athletes. William taught the men at the YMCA the rules of basketball, but he noticed that some men didn't participate as eagerly as others. Men who were older or weren't very athletic couldn't keep up with all the running or the physical contact of basketball. William wanted to think of a game like basketball where everyone, no matter their age or ability, would participate equally.

William combined ideas from various sports like handball, tennis, and badminton to create a new sport. He wanted the game to be easily played in any gym or open air. Next, he created some ground rules and tried to figure out which ball was best to use. After trying balls for several other sports, William hadn't found the right fit. So, he asked a new company, A.G. Spalding & Bros, to create a new ball for his sport.

Originally, he called the sport "mintonette," but later a friend suggested he call it "volleyball" and the name stuck! William kept improving the rules until 1896, when volleyball was added to the first official YMCA athletic handbook. The game instantly became popular! In 1964 volleyball was introduced to the Summer Olympics.

William was happy to have invented a sport that so many people enjoyed. The next time you see some friends or family playing volleyball, join in and think about William Morgan!

William Wilberforce was a British politician who played a key role in making slavery illegal. He was born in 1759 in Yorkshire during a time when Europeans took people from Africa and made them slaves. It's hard for us to believe that anyone could think that slavery was okay, but back in those days a lot of people did. By owning slaves, masters made a lot of money, which made it easy to ignore the truth.

William grew up going to a church where the pastor was an ex-slave trader named John Newton. Seeing firsthand the evils of slavery, John Newton became an abolitionist, which is someone who worked to bring an end to slavery. He became a mentor to William, who became a Christian as a young man. Together they founded the Anti-Slavery Society and taught that every person has great value. Their Christian faith was the driving force behind their dedication to abolishing slavery.

William said, "Life as we know it, with all its ups and downs, will soon be over. We all will give an accounting to God of how we have lived." William held a position of power. He was a part of the British government, in the House of Commons. Their job was, and still is, to make laws. Often, he gave speeches trying to persuade the other lawmakers to end the slave trade. Newspapers said his speeches were some of the best anyone had ever given, but most of the lawmakers voted against him. They thought the slave trade was making too much money to end it. William did not give up!

He said, "We are too young to realize that certain things are impossible… so we will do them anyway." He worked and spoke for 18 years without seeing any change in the law.

Finally, the British government ended the slave trade, which stopped shipment of slaves from Africa but didn't free people who were already slaves. So, William and his friends kept working. At last, a law passed to completely end slavery in Britain in 1833, just three days before William died. He lived to see his dream come true. It would still take years of hard work and sacrifice by many people to make slavery illegal around the world.

We learn from William Wilberforce that we might work for a long time without seeing the fruits of our labor, but the hard work is still worth it! When the going gets tough, remember William Wilberforce!

William Carney was the first Black American to receive a Medal of Honor. He was born a slave in 1840 in Virginia. His father escaped slavery through the Underground Railroad and worked until he was able to buy freedom for his wife and son. After paying for their freedom, the Carney family moved to Massachusetts where William was educated and dreamed of becoming a minister.

But the American Civil War changed that dream for him. Instead, he felt called by God to serve in the Union Army, in the first all-Black Regiment. Because of his education and leadership skills, William quickly became a sergeant. His regiment first saw combat in South Carolina in 1863 when they charged Fort Wagner.

The colonel and flag-bearer were mortally wounded in battle, and as William saw the American flag fall, he rushed to keep it from touching the ground. Though he was wounded in several places, he planted the flag in high ground during the heat of battle. Reinforcements arrived to withdraw the wounded troops and William carried the flag out. His heroism inspired his comrades to remain strong.

Proudly, he exclaimed, "Boys, the old flag never touched the ground!" Afterward, he was honorably discharged from the Army because of his wounds. Thirty-seven years after showing such bravery in battle, William was awarded the highest military honor, the Congressional Medal of Honor.

He left a legacy of patriotism despite the many challenges he faced as a Black American born into slavery. When you handle a flag, never let it touch the ground and think about patriotic William Carney!

William "Bill" Gates is an American business leader, entrepreneur, and philanthropist. Born in 1955 in Seattle, Washington, little Bill's mother would often take him along when she volunteered at community functions. She influenced him to be charitable with the wealth he would one day gain. As a boy, he was competitive and loved to play games like Risk and Monopoly.

Although his childhood was happy, his parents worried that he was becoming withdrawn and a loner. Bill was often bored in school until he found something that fascinated him - computers. He spent all his free time learning all he could about them. In high school, he created a tic-tac-toe game on a BASIC computer program that allowed users to play against the computer.

When he was 15, he and his friend Paul Allen developed a program that monitored traffic in Seattle. Together, they made a big profit from the program and made a goal to start their own computer company. This was his first step in becoming an entrepreneur, which is someone who takes big risks to organize a business.

Bill's parents wanted him to go to college to become a lawyer. After high school, he was accepted to Harvard University and pursued a career in law, as his parents wished. But Bill was much more interested in computers! After two years of college, he dropped out to pursue his passion - his business, Microsoft, with Paul Allen. It turns out he made the right choice. Microsoft took off and Bill Gates became the richest man in the world. He learned from both his successes and failures as a businessman.

He said, "Success is a lousy teacher. It seduces smart people into thinking they can't lose." Bill and his ex-wife Melinda French Gates work together as philanthropists, which means they donate generously to wonderful causes. The Bill & Melinda Gates Foundation has donated billions of dollars to health and education in developing countries. Over the years, he has cut back time spent at Microsoft to spend more time helping others through his foundation.

The next time you use a program in Microsoft Office, Windows, or play on an *Xbox*, think about Bill Gates, the man who started it all!

William Henry Cling was a Black American inventor. He was born in 1866 to former slaves in South Carolina. When he grew up, William became a barber who had a knack for thinking of great ideas and turning them into useful inventions. Interestingly, none of his inventions were related to his profession as a barber.

In 1896 he invented a mechanical device used to keep track of the number of people at a place. This invention, called the passenger register, was used at theaters or public events like fairs. It was a much better system than counting people and tallying with paper and pencil, like the previous system. Mechanical handheld tally counters are used to this day!

Nine years later, he invented a railway safety device to save people's lives! Frequently trains would have head-on or rear collisions if they were on the same track. He knew that there must be a way to fix this problem. So, William Henry Cling set emergency brakes in the trains to prevent this. Later he thought of an idea to put wires in shoelaces. With this new design, the laces could be tied with a simple twist.

A few years later, he came up with a way to make life easier for people who were bed-ridden. He noticed that people who had to stay in bed because of injuries or sickness couldn't sit upright without great effort by their caretakers. So, William designed a bed which could be folded into an upright position. These days, modern technology has improved these beds, and hospitals have them in every room!

Inventors make it their goal to make life easier. Think about ways to make life easier and turn those ideas into inventions! Then you will be like creative and clever William Henry Cling!

William Shakespeare was the most well-known playwright and poet the world has ever known. He was born in Stratford-upon-Avon in England in 1564. His plays have been performed worldwide for hundreds of years, but surprisingly little is known about him as a person.

Old church records show that William was baptized as an infant, the third of six children to upper-middle class parents. In 1582 he married Anne Hathaway, a woman from a town nearby. Together they had three children. Sadly, one of his children died when he was 11 of unknown causes.

For many years after the birth of his children, there are no records of William Shakespeare at all. Historians can only make guesses about his upbringing, education and life experiences that turned him into such an outstanding writer.

The next record of him is in the early 1590's, when he worked as a manager and playwright for an acting company called the Lord Chamberlain's Men, later called the King's Men. He wrote and published 15 plays while working for this company. Then he and his business partners built their own theater, which they called the Globe.

While at the Globe, he wrote 22 more plays. Queen Elizabeth I was a supporter of theater and she attended William's plays. During his life, he enjoyed success in his career. After his death, his works became widespread, and he became the most famous writer ever to live. His plays are still loved because they always have lessons for us. William Shakespeare's characters capture complicated human emotions and struggles in a timeless way.

William Shakespeare wrote these famous lines in his plays:

"Love all, trust a few, do wrong to none."
-*All's Well That Ends Well*

"The world's a stage, and all the men and women merely players."
-*As You Like It*

"The course of true love never did run smooth."
-*A Midsummer Night's Dream*

"It is a wise father that knows his own child."
-*The Merchant of Venice*

"Suspicion always haunts the guilty mind."
-*Henry VI*

"No legacy is so rich as honesty."
-*All's Well That Ends Well*

"One touch of nature makes the whole world kin."
-*Troilus and Cressida*

"All that glitters is not gold."
-*The Merchant of Venice*

"To thine own self be true."
-*Hamlet*

William Shakespeare is quoted more than any other author. As you grow and learn, you will hear smart people quote him. Listen for those quotes and remember the literary genius, William Shakespeare!

This page is all about you!

_____ was born on

_____

As a baby, William _____

_____

As a little boy, William _____

_____

William is especially good at _____

_____

William is often described as _____

_____

William makes people laugh when he _____

_____

One day William would like to _____

_____

This page for making a self-portrait. A self-portrait is a picture of you, drawn by you!

Bibliography

"About William." *Williamkamkwamba.org*. 2013. Web. 27 Apr. 2020.

Biography.com editors. "William Shakespeare Biography." *The biography.com website*. A&E Television Networks, 11 Aug. 2017. Web. 21 Sep. 2018

Encyclopaedia Britannica editors. "Bill Gates." *Encyclopaedia Britannica*. Encyclopaedia Britannica, inc. 11 Mar. 2024 Web. 13 Mar. 2024.

Encyclopaedia Britannica editors. "William Wilberforce." *Encyclopaedia Britannica*. Encyclopaedia Britannica, inc. 20 Aug. 2020. Web. 27 Sep. 2020.

Helm, Matt. "Carney, William H. (1840-1908)." *BlackPast.org*. BlackPast. 2017. Web. 26 Sep. 2018

Wikipedia contributors. "William Harvey Carney." *Wikipedia, The Free Encyclopedia*. Wikipedia, The Free Encyclopedia, 6 Sep. 2018. Web. 27 Sep. 2018.

Wikipedia contributors. "William Henry Cling." *Wikipedia, The Free Encyclopedia*. Wikipedia, The Free Encyclopedia, 18 Oct. 2017. Web. 24 Sep. 2018

Wikipedia contributors. "Bill Gates." *Wikipedia, The Free Encyclopedia*. Wikipedia, The Free Encyclopedia, 10 Mar. 2024. Web. 12 Mar. 2024

Wikipedia contributors. "William Kamkwamba." *Wikipedia, The Free Encyclopedia*. Wikipedia, The Free Encyclopedia, 14 Apr. 2020. Web. 27 Apr. 2020

Wikipedia contributors. "William G. Morgan." *Wikipedia, The Free Encyclopedia*. Wikipedia, The Free Encyclopedia, 3 Sep. 2018. Web. 27 Sep. 2018.

Wikipedia contributors. "William." *Wikipedia, The Free Encyclopedia*. Wikipedia, The Free Encyclopedia, 19 Sep. 2018. Web. 20 Sep. 2018.

www.ingramcontent.com/pod-product-compliance
Lightning Source LLC
Chambersburg PA
CBHW042111040426
42448CB00002B/230